Mindful Saving Techniques: How to Achieve Financial Balance and Wellness

Transform Your Money Management with Mindful Spending and Psychology-Based Practices

Jade Harper

Contents

Foreword

Money: it's that one thing we all deal with, but nobody really likes to talk about. It's a little like that overly ambitious sourdough starter everyone tried to maintain during lockdown—messy, complicated, and sometimes just plain overwhelming. But here's the thing: our relationship with money doesn't have to feel like a chore, and it definitely doesn't have to come with a side of stress-induced heartburn.

This book, *Mindful Saving Techniques: How to Achieve Financial Balance and Wellness*, isn't about shaming your spending habits (yes, that third delivery app order in a single weekend is between you and your conscience). Instead, it's about approaching money with the kind of mindfulness and intention that will make you wonder why you didn't start sooner. Think of it as a permission slip to stop panicking over finances and start building a relationship with your money that feels...well, healthier.

Here's the catch: money isn't just numbers and spreadsheets. It's emotions, memories, and sometimes a healthy sprinkle of irrational fears (who hasn't felt a pang of guilt for splurging on something totally unnecessary?). The good news is, with the help of mindfulness, you can actually unravel those tricky feelings, take back control, and even feel a little proud of how you handle your finances.

This book blends practical advice with a touch of psychology and a whole lot of common sense. It's not here to lecture you or tell you to skip the things that bring you joy (looking at you, fancy coffee drinkers). Instead, it's here to show you how to save, spend, and invest in ways that align with what truly matters to you—without the guilt or sleepless nights.

So, if your money habits could use a little TLC (and whose couldn't?), you're in the right place. Get ready to laugh, reflect, and maybe even breathe a sigh of relief as you navigate a more mindful approach to your financial life. This isn't just a book; it's a guide to finding peace, balance, and maybe even a little fun in the way you manage your money.

Let's get started, shall we?

Cheers to a brighter financial future,

Jade Harper

Chapter 1
The Foundations of Money Mindfulness

Let's start with the basics. Money: you earn it, you spend it, and sometimes, you frantically check your banking app hoping your rent didn't go through *just yet*. Sound familiar? Don't worry, you're in good company. Most of us have a love-hate relationship with money—it's a bit like that friend who always wants to split the bill evenly even though they ordered the lobster. But what if I told you it doesn't have to be that way?

Welcome to *money mindfulness*. It's like regular mindfulness, but instead of sitting in a lotus position and thinking about your breath, you'll be sitting with your budget and thinking about why you suddenly "needed" that electric pasta maker (spoiler: you didn't).

This chapter is about laying the groundwork for a healthier, more balanced relationship with money. Because let's face it, whether you have millions in the bank or just enough to cover that questionable subscription you forgot to cancel, your financial well-being affects your overall peace of mind. So, let's dive into the psychology of money, explore the magic of mindfulness, and get real about the emotional baggage we all bring to our wallets.

. . .

The Psychology of Money: It's Not You, It's Your Brain

Here's a fun fact: your brain has been sabotaging your finances for years. That impulse purchase you made last week? Blame your emotions. The time you saved up for something practical but spent it all on a last-minute weekend getaway? That's your brain chasing short-term happiness instead of long-term stability.

The truth is, money isn't just numbers and spreadsheets—it's deeply personal. Our beliefs about money are shaped by our upbringing, experiences, and the weird cultural messages we've absorbed over time (who decided "treat yourself" was a financial strategy, anyway?).

Maybe you grew up hearing things like, "Money doesn't grow on trees!" or, "We can't afford that!" Or maybe your family avoided the topic of money altogether, leaving you to piece things together from sitcoms and cereal commercials. Either way, those early lessons stick with us, shaping how we earn, spend, and save.

Now, I know what you're thinking: *Great, so my money issues are my parents' fault?* Well, kind of. But the good news is, we're here to rewrite that narrative. And the first step? Becoming aware of your current money mindset.

Mindfulness to the Rescue: A Superpower for Your Finances

Let's talk about mindfulness for a second. No, you don't need to light incense or chant affirmations to make it work for your wallet (unless you want to, in which case, go for it). Mindfulness is just about paying attention—really paying attention—to what you're doing, how you're feeling, and why.

Applied to money, mindfulness can:

- **Reduce stress.** Picture this: instead of panicking every time you see a bill, you approach it calmly, with a plan. Feels good, right?

- **Increase awareness.** Ever checked your bank account and thought, *Wait, when did I spend $100 at that home goods store?* Mindfulness helps you stay present in your spending so there are no surprises later.
- **Empower your choices.** When you're mindful, you make intentional decisions that align with your goals, rather than just reacting to every sale email or social media ad.

In short, mindfulness helps you take control of your finances, one thoughtful decision at a time.

Exercise: What's Your Money Story?

Okay, time for a little self-reflection. Grab a notebook (or the back of an old receipt) and answer these questions:

1. **What's your earliest memory of money?**
2. Was it the thrill of finding a $5 bill on the sidewalk? Or the sting of being told you couldn't have that toy at the store?
3. **What messages about money did you grow up with?**
4. Did your family emphasize saving, spending, or pretending money didn't exist?
5. **What do you believe about money now?**
6. Be honest: Do you think money is a source of security, stress, or something else entirely?
7. **What do you want to change about your relationship with money?**
8. Maybe you want to stop impulse buying or feel less anxious about your finances. Write it down.

Setting Intentions: Your Money Mindfulness Mantra

Now that you've done a little soul-searching, it's time to set an intention for this journey. What do you want to get out of this whole "money mindfulness" thing? Maybe it's a sense of balance, less financial stress, or even just the ability to stick to a budget without crying.

Write your intention somewhere you'll see it often—on a sticky note, your phone background, or even on your fridge (money mindfulness and snack mindfulness go hand in hand).

What's Next?

Congratulations! You've taken the first step toward a more mindful relationship with your money. You've reflected on your money story, set an intention, and hopefully cracked a smile or two along the way. In the next chapter, we'll dive deeper into your "money story" and explore how your past is still shaping your financial present.

But for now, take a deep breath. You're doing great. And remember: the journey to financial wellness isn't about being perfect; it's about being present.

Let's keep going, one intentional step at a time.

* * *

TAKE ACTION

Challenge: Spend 5 minutes each day for a week reflecting on how money makes you feel—stress, empowerment, or something else. Write your thoughts in a journal.

* * *

MILESTONE:

Celebrate by summarizing your reflections and identifying one key area where you want to grow financially.

* * *

JOURNALLING PROMPTS:

- How do I currently feel about money? What emotions come up when I think about my finances?
- What does financial wellness mean to me, and how would I know if I achieved it?
- What intention can I set for my financial mindfulness journey?

Chapter 2
Understanding Your Money Story

You know how every great superhero has an origin story? Bruce Wayne had that bat-filled cave, Peter Parker had the radioactive spider, and we all have...money. Okay, so it's not exactly the stuff of comic books, but your money story is just as powerful when it comes to shaping your life.

Whether you realize it or not, your relationship with money—how you think about it, manage it, and even stress over it—is deeply rooted in your past. Your earliest memories, family habits, and cultural messages have all woven together into a narrative that plays out every time you open your wallet or swipe your card.

But here's the kicker: just like a superhero, you have the power to rewrite your origin story. And that's what this chapter is all about.

The First Chapter of Your Money Story: Childhood Memories

Let's rewind to when you were a kid. Think about your first encounter with money. Maybe it was when you got your first allowance or saw your parents arguing over a bill. Or perhaps it was that moment of pure joy when you found a shiny coin on the playground and immediately spent it on candy.

Whatever it was, those early experiences were more than just moments—they were lessons. You were soaking in cues about what money means and how it should be handled.

Exercise: Digging Into Your Money Memories

Take a moment to reflect on these questions. Write down whatever comes to mind—it doesn't have to be pretty, just honest:

1. What's your earliest memory of money?
2. How did your family talk about money when you were growing up? Did they talk about it at all?
3. Was money a source of stress, joy, or something else in your household?
4. How did those experiences make you feel about money back then?

Now look at your answers. Notice any patterns? These memories aren't just nostalgic—they've likely influenced how you handle money today.

Your Inherited Financial Beliefs

Let's talk about hand-me-downs. No, not the kind of hand-me-downs that involve your cousin's questionable fashion choices. We're talking about financial beliefs.

You probably inherited some money habits from your family—whether you meant to or not. Maybe your parents were big savers, always looking for a deal and putting every extra penny into a rainy-day fund. Or maybe they were spenders, living for the moment and dealing with the consequences later.

These habits, consciously or not, have a way of sticking. If your family treated money as something scarce, you might now feel anxious every time you spend. If they saw money as a tool for enjoyment, you might find yourself leaning toward impulse buys.

Exercise: Mapping Your Inherited Money Habits

Let's dig a little deeper:

1. What were some common phrases or sayings about money in your household? (Examples: "Money doesn't grow on trees" or "You can't take it with you.")
2. How did your parents or guardians approach saving and spending? Were they cautious, carefree, or somewhere in between?
3. How do you see those habits reflected in your own financial behavior today?

The goal here isn't to assign blame—this isn't about shaking your fist at your parents for not letting you get the expensive sneakers. It's about understanding where your beliefs come from so you can decide whether they still serve you.

Cultural Messages and the Money Myth Machine

As if your family wasn't enough, society had to get in on the action too. From ads that tell you happiness comes in the form of a new car to social media influencers who somehow make luxury vacations look like daily errands, cultural messages about money are everywhere.

These messages often create myths about what money should mean:

- **Money equals success.** If you're not rolling in it, you're not "winning" at life.
- **Spending equals happiness.** Because what's better than retail therapy after a bad day?

- **Debt equals failure.** Even though the average person has more debt than they'd like to admit.

Exercise: Spotting the Myths

Think about the cultural messages that have influenced you. Ask yourself:

1. What do I believe money "says" about me?
2. What advertisements, social media posts, or societal norms have shaped my views on spending and saving?
3. Are these beliefs true, or are they just myths I've internalized over time?

Reframing the Narrative

Now that you've unearthed some of the roots of your money story, it's time to rewrite the script. Just because you grew up with certain beliefs or absorbed cultural messages doesn't mean you're stuck with them.

Reframing is about questioning the stories you've told yourself and replacing them with ones that better align with your values.

Techniques for Reframing Your Money Narrative

1. **Challenge Your Beliefs.** For every negative thought about money ("I'll never be good with it" or "I'm not capable of saving"), ask yourself: Is this actually true, or is it just a story I've been telling myself?
2. **Replace Scarcity with Abundance.** If you grew up believing there's never enough money, try reframing that to "I have the ability to create financial security."
3. **Embrace Your Power.** Instead of feeling like money controls you, remind yourself that you're the one making the decisions.

9

4. **Visualize Your Ideal Money Story.** Imagine what a healthy relationship with money looks like for you. Write it down as if it's already true: "I handle my money with confidence and ease."

Moving Forward

Your money story is a key part of who you are, but it doesn't define your future. By understanding where your beliefs come from, recognizing which ones are holding you back, and actively working to reframe them, you're already on the path to a healthier financial mindset.

In the next chapter, we'll take all this self-awareness and put it into action by building a budget that doesn't feel like a punishment. Trust me, budgeting can actually be...dare I say it? Fun. But for now, give yourself credit for doing the hard work of looking inward.

You're rewriting your money story—and that's the ultimate super-hero move.

* * *

TAKE ACTION

Understanding Your Money Story

Challenge: Write down three formative money memories from your childhood and note how they shaped your current financial mindset.

* * *

MILESTONE:

Share your insights with a trusted friend or journal about how understanding these memories can help you move forward.

* * *

JOURNALLING PROMPTS:

- What are three memories from my childhood that shaped
  how I think about money?
- Are there any financial beliefs or habits I've inherited
  that I want to challenge or change?
- How would my financial life look if I rewrote one
  unhelpful money narrative?

Chapter 3
Building a Mindful Budget

L et's be real: the word *budget* doesn't exactly inspire joy. For many, it conjures up images of spreadsheets, endless math, and the heartbreaking realization that maybe we shouldn't have splurged on that third delivery meal last week. But here's the thing: budgeting doesn't have to feel like a financial punishment.

If the thought of budgeting makes you groan, you're not alone. The traditional narrative around budgeting often paints it as a tool for deprivation—a way to say "no" to all the fun stuff and "yes" to...well, boring stuff like bills. But what if I told you that budgeting, when done mindfully, isn't about restriction? It's about freedom.

Imagine this: instead of wondering where your money went at the end of the month, you *know* where it's going. Instead of feeling guilty about a night out with friends, you've already accounted for it. A mindful budget isn't about cutting out everything you love; it's about spending in ways that align with your values and long-term goals.

When you approach budgeting with this perspective, it transforms from a chore to a tool of empowerment. It's no longer about "not being allowed" to do something—it's about making intentional choices that reflect what's truly important to you. It brings clarity to your financial decisions, reduces unnecessary stress, and helps you prioritize what really matters.

So, if you've ever felt like budgeting was the enemy, take a deep breath. This chapter is here to show you that building a mindful budget isn't just doable—it's liberating. And it might even be a little... dare I say it? Fun. Let's dive in.

Section 1: Needs, Wants, and True Desires

When it comes to money, not all spending is created equal. Some expenses are absolutely necessary (hello, rent), while others are nice-to-haves (yes, that fancy latte counts), and then there are the purchases that truly add value to your life. Understanding the difference between these categories is the first step in building a mindful budget that reflects your priorities.

Understanding the Categories

Needs: The Non-Negotiables

Let's start with the basics—your *needs*. These are the essentials that keep the lights on, a roof over your head, and food in your belly. Think of them as the building blocks of your financial stability.

Examples of needs include:

- Housing (rent or mortgage)
- Utilities (electricity, water, internet, etc.)
- Groceries
- Transportation (public transit, gas, car payments)

- Insurance (health, car, etc.)

Needs are the foundation of your budget. They're non-negotiable, but that doesn't mean they have to drain your wallet unnecessarily. Being mindful about how you fulfill these needs—like finding ways to save on groceries or energy bills—can free up resources for other priorities.

Wants: The Fun Stuff

Ah, *wants*. These are the expenses that make life enjoyable but aren't strictly necessary for survival. Think of them as the cherry on top of your financial sundae.

Examples of wants include:

- Entertainment (Netflix, movie tickets, concerts)
- Dining out or ordering takeout
- Subscriptions (streaming services, fitness apps)
- Non-essential shopping (clothes, gadgets, home décor)

Wants often get a bad rap in the budgeting world, but let's be clear: spending on wants isn't inherently bad. In fact, these are the things that often bring joy and relaxation to our lives. The key is being mindful about how much you're spending on wants and whether they're truly adding value.

True Desires: The Meaningful Splurges

This is where things get interesting. *True desires* are a step beyond basic wants—they're the expenses that align with your values and bring lasting satisfaction. These are the things you'll remember fondly, rather than regret after a week.

Examples of true desires might include:

- Taking a class or pursuing a hobby you're passionate about.

- Investing in experiences, like travel or time with loved ones.
- Saving for a future goal, like a dream home or career change.
- Supporting causes or communities that matter to you.

True desires are deeply personal, and they often bring a sense of fulfillment that fleeting wants can't match. When you prioritize true desires, your spending feels more intentional and rewarding.

Exercise: Categorizing Your Expenses

Let's put this into practice. Grab your last month's bank statement, a notebook, or a budgeting app, and take a close look at your spending. Create a table with three columns: **Needs, Wants, and True Desires.**

Here's an example:

True Desires

Rent/mortgage
Coffee shop visits
Weekend getaway with family
Groceries
Streaming subscription
Donations to a cause you care about
Utilities
New clothing
Online art class

Now, categorize each expense. Be honest with yourself—don't try to justify that impulse purchase as a "true desire" unless it genuinely aligns with your values.

Reflect on the Patterns

Once you've categorized everything, ask yourself:

- Are you spending too much on fleeting wants and not enough on true desires?
- Are your needs taking up more of your budget than you realized?
- Are there areas where you can cut back to focus on what truly matters?

This exercise isn't about shaming yourself for past spending—it's about gaining awareness so you can make more intentional choices moving forward.

Reframing Wants

Let's talk about wants for a moment. These are the "fun" expenses that often get blamed for blowing budgets. But not all wants are created equal. Some bring genuine happiness, while others offer only fleeting satisfaction.

The Question to Ask Yourself

The next time you're tempted by a want, pause and ask:

- Will this purchase bring me lasting happiness, or will it end up gathering dust?

For example:

- That trendy gadget might seem exciting now, but will it still spark joy in a month?
- A dinner out with friends, on the other hand, might create memories you'll cherish for years.

The goal here isn't to eliminate wants altogether—it's to focus on the ones that genuinely add value to your life.

Conclusion: Aligning Spending with Values

By distinguishing between needs, wants, and true desires, you're setting the foundation for a budget that's not just functional but also meaningful. When you understand where your money is going and why, you can spend with confidence, knowing your finances reflect what's truly important to you.

In the next section, we'll take these insights and build a budget that honors both your present needs and your future goals. But for now, take a moment to celebrate the fact that you're already making more mindful financial choices—and that's a win worth savoring.

Section 2: Setting Up a Mindful Budget

Now that we've categorized your expenses into needs, wants, and true desires, it's time to build a budget that works for you—not one that feels like financial handcuffs. A mindful budget isn't about perfection; it's about clarity, balance, and making choices that align with your values. Think of it as your personal money map, guiding you toward your goals without taking all the joy out of spending.

Core Principles of a Mindful Budget

Flexibility: Budgets Aren't Meant to Be Set in Stone

Life happens. Your car breaks down, your best friend suddenly gets engaged, or you discover a new passion for pottery. A mindful budget allows for adjustments without sending you into a spiral of guilt or panic. The key is to approach these changes with awareness and intention, rather than treating them as "failures."

Balance: Address Both Present and Future Needs

A good budget is like a well-balanced meal—it satisfies today's hunger while ensuring you're not raiding the fridge at midnight. Allocate funds for both immediate necessities (needs) and your aspirations (savings and true desires).

Intentionality: Give Every Dollar a Purpose

Mindful budgeting means knowing exactly where your money is going and why. Instead of letting your dollars wander off into the unknown, assign each one a task—whether that's paying a bill, funding your dream vacation, or treating yourself to a well-earned splurge.

Breaking Down the Budget

Let's break your budget into four key components:

1. Income: Know Your Monthly Net Income

Start by calculating your monthly net income (that's your take-home pay after taxes and deductions). If your income varies (hello, freelancers!), use a conservative estimate based on your average monthly earnings.

2. Fixed Expenses: Cover the Essentials

These are your recurring, non-negotiable costs—your financial foundation. Examples include:

- Rent or mortgage payments
- Utilities (electricity, water, internet)
- Insurance (health, car, etc.)
- Debt payments (student loans, credit cards)

Calculate the total amount of your fixed expenses and ensure it fits comfortably within your income.

3. Variable Expenses: Adaptable Spending Categories

These expenses change from month to month, but they're still important to track. Examples include:

- Groceries
- Transportation (gas, public transit)
- Dining out
- Entertainment (streaming subscriptions, hobbies)

Being mindful of variable expenses allows you to adjust spending in response to your goals or unexpected events.

4. Savings and Goals: Prioritize Your Future

Your future self will thank you for prioritizing savings. Divide this category into two parts:

- **Short-term goals:** Emergency fund, upcoming trips, or holiday gifts.
- **Long-term goals:** Retirement, buying a home, or starting a business.

Aim to save at least 20% of your income, but adjust based on your circumstances and aspirations.

Exercise: Creating Your Budget Blueprint

Grab a notebook, spreadsheet, or budgeting app, and let's get started on your mindful budget.

Step 1: Use This Sample Template

Your Monthly Amount

Needs (Fixed + Variable) 50%
Wants 30%
Savings & Goals 20%

Step 2: Fill in the Blanks

- Start with your net income. Example: If you take home $3,000 per month, calculate 50% for needs ($1,500), 30% for wants ($900), and 20% for savings ($600).
- Adjust percentages if needed, based on your financial goals and priorities.

Step 3: Assign Specific Amounts

Break down each category into subcategories. For example:

- **Needs:** $1,000 for rent, $300 for utilities, $200 for groceries.
- **Wants:** $100 for dining out, $100 for entertainment, $200 for discretionary shopping.
- **Savings:** $300 for an emergency fund, $300 for a vacation fund.

Step 4: Reflect and Adjust

Once your blueprint is complete, ask yourself:

- Does this budget align with my values and goals?
- Am I over-allocating to wants at the expense of savings or needs?
- Can I adjust anything to better reflect what matters most to me?

The Magic of Percentages

If you're not sure where to start, the **50/30/20 rule** is a great guideline:

- **50% for Needs:** Cover your essentials.
- **30% for Wants:** Enjoy life without overindulging.
- **20% for Savings:** Secure your future.

Of course, these percentages can and should be customized based on your individual circumstances. If you're working to pay off debt, you might reduce spending on wants to funnel more money toward your goals.

Final Thoughts on Building Your Blueprint

Your budget is your financial compass—it helps you navigate life with clarity and purpose. Remember, it's not a rigid set of rules but a living document that evolves with your needs and goals.

In the next section, we'll dive into mindful spending and saving techniques to make sure your budget works for you—not the other way around. For now, take pride in the fact that you've taken the first step toward a more intentional financial future. Your budget isn't just a tool—it's a reflection of your values and dreams.

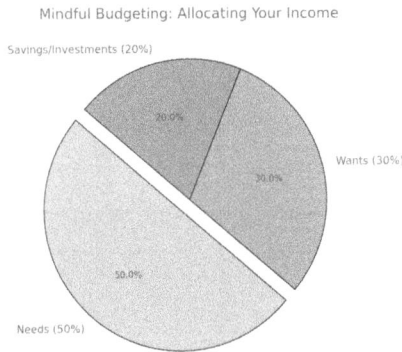

Mindful Budgeting Pie Chart: Displays the "50/30/20" budgeting rule, emphasizing the allocation of income into needs, wants, and savings/investments.

25

Section 3: Mindful Spending and Conscious Saving Techniques

A budget is only as effective as your ability to stick to it, but sticking to it doesn't mean giving up everything fun or living in perpetual sacrifice mode. It's about spending and saving with intention—making choices that reflect your values and priorities. Let's explore how to master both sides of this financial coin.

Mindful Spending Tips

Spending money can be surprisingly emotional. Whether it's a little pick-me-up on a tough day or a splurge to celebrate something big, purchases are often tied to how we feel in the moment. Mindful spending helps you step back and think before swiping your card, ensuring your purchases align with your values.

1. Pause Before Purchases

When you're about to buy something, ask yourself:

- "Does this align with my values?"

- "Will this bring me lasting satisfaction, or is it a fleeting desire?"

This simple pause can prevent impulse purchases and help you feel more confident about where your money is going.

2. Use the "48-Hour Rule"

For non-essential purchases, implement a 48-hour waiting period. If you still want the item after two days and it fits within your budget, go ahead. But chances are, you'll often find that the urge passes, saving you from buyer's remorse.

3. Track Spending Daily or Weekly

Tracking your expenses in real-time keeps you aware of your financial habits. Whether you use a notebook, an app, or an Excel sheet, recording your spending helps you:

- Spot patterns (like that sneaky daily coffee habit).
- Stay within your budget limits.
- Feel more in control of your finances.

Conscious Saving Techniques

Saving money often feels like a chore, but it doesn't have to be. When approached mindfully, saving becomes an act of self-care—something you do to support your future self and the goals you hold dear.

1. Automate Your Savings

Set up automatic transfers to your savings account as soon as you get paid. Automating eliminates the temptation to spend that money elsewhere and makes saving a consistent habit without extra effort.

2. Set Savings Goals Tied to Meaningful Aspirations

Saving is easier when you know what you're saving for. Instead of a vague goal like "save more," be specific:

- "Save $1,000 for an emergency fund by June."
- "Put aside $300 per month for a family vacation."

- "Build a $5,000 fund for a career transition in two years."

Knowing *why* you're saving makes it more motivating and purposeful.

3. Celebrate Small Wins

Each time you hit a milestone—no matter how small—take a moment to celebrate. Whether it's reaching your first $500 in an emergency fund or resisting an impulse buy to stay on track, recognizing your progress keeps you motivated for the long haul.

Exercise: The "Spending Filter"

The Spending Filter is a checklist to help you evaluate purchases before making them. Here's how it works:

Step 1: Ask Yourself These Questions

1. **Is this a need, want, or true desire?**
   - Needs are essential, like groceries or rent.
   - Wants are nice-to-haves but not urgent.
   - True desires are meaningful expenses that align with your values.
2. **How will this purchase impact my budget and goals?**
   - Will it push you over budget for the month?
   - Could that money be better spent or saved toward a priority goal?
3. **Will I still value this in a month?**
   - Is this purchase a fleeting whim, or will it bring lasting happiness or utility?

Step 2: Reflect on Your Answers

If the purchase doesn't pass the Spending Filter, give yourself permission to walk away. You're not saying "no" to spending entirely—you're saying "yes" to intentionality and your bigger goals.

Step 3: Practice and Review

Use the Spending Filter regularly to build the habit of mindful spending. Over time, you'll notice fewer impulse buys and more purchases that truly add value to your life.

Final Thoughts on Spending and Saving Mindfully

Mindful spending and saving aren't about deprivation—they're about aligning your financial habits with your values and goals. When you pause before purchases, automate your savings, and stay focused on what truly matters, you create a sense of balance and empowerment in your financial life.

In the next section, we'll explore how to keep your budget on track through regular check-ins and reflections. But for now, take a moment to appreciate this: every mindful choice you make today is a step toward a brighter, more intentional financial future.

Section 4: Monthly Check-In Exercises

A budget is like a garden—it needs regular care and attention to thrive. Without check-ins, even the most carefully crafted budget can veer off course, leaving you frustrated and unsure where your money went. Monthly check-ins are your chance to reflect, recalibrate, and celebrate progress. They're not about judging yourself but about learning and growing with your financial habits.

Why Monthly Check-Ins Matter

Think of your budget as a living, breathing thing. Life happens—unexpected expenses pop up, priorities shift, and sometimes, that sale on concert tickets is just too good to pass up. That's why regular check-ins are essential:

- **Prevents Budgets from Feeling Stagnant:** A static budget can feel restrictive. Monthly reviews ensure your budget evolves with your needs and circumstances.
- **Provides Opportunities to Adjust:** Did you overspend in one area but save in another? Check-ins let you make tweaks so you're always on track.

- **Keeps You Connected to Your Values:** Regular reflection helps you see whether your spending aligns with your priorities, allowing you to course-correct if needed.

Steps for a Mindful Monthly Review

A monthly check-in doesn't have to be complicated or time-consuming. Set aside 30 minutes at the end of each month, grab your favorite beverage, and follow these simple steps:

1. Review the Past Month's Spending

Look at your expenses for the month and ask yourself:

- Were there any surprises or unplanned expenses?
- Did you stick to your budget categories?
- Are there areas where you consistently overspend or underspend?

This step is about awareness, not perfection. If you notice patterns—like spending more on dining out than you planned—acknowledge them without guilt. Awareness is the first step toward change.

2. Assess Progress Toward Savings Goals

Check your progress on short-term and long-term goals:

- Are you on track to hit your targets?
- If not, what adjustments can you make to get back on track?

Celebrating progress, no matter how small, keeps you motivated. Even if you're not where you want to be yet, every step forward is worth acknowledging.

3. Reflect on How Spending Aligned With Your Values

Take a moment to think about your spending choices:

- Did you prioritize true desires over fleeting wants?
- Were there any purchases that didn't bring as much joy or utility as you expected?
- How did your spending contribute to the life you want to build?

This reflection helps you stay connected to your bigger goals and make adjustments for the coming month.

Exercise: The Budget Reflection Journal

Your monthly check-in is the perfect time to journal about your financial journey. Reflection not only provides clarity but also reinforces positive habits.

Step 1: Write About One Spending Choice You're Proud Of

Think back over the past month and identify a spending decision that aligned with your values. Maybe you resisted an impulse buy, prioritized a true desire, or found a creative way to save. Write about how it felt and why it mattered to you.

Step 2: Write About One Spending Choice You'd Handle Differently

No one's perfect, and that's okay. Reflect on a decision you'd like to approach differently next time. What led to that choice? What did you learn from it? This isn't about beating yourself up—it's about identifying opportunities for growth.

Step 3: Practice Gratitude

Take a moment to appreciate what your budget has allowed you to achieve this month. Did you pay off a bill, contribute to your savings, or enjoy a meaningful experience? Gratitude keeps you motivated and focused on the positive aspects of your financial journey.

Final Thoughts on Monthly Check-Ins

Monthly check-ins are like having a conversation with your finances. They help you understand what's working, what's not, and how to move forward with intention. By regularly reflecting on your spending and savings, you stay connected to your goals and values, making adjustments as needed to stay on track.

Next month, you might find yourself making even more mindful choices—and that's the beauty of this process. It's not about perfection; it's about progress. So, schedule your first check-in, grab that notebook, and start building a habit that will keep your finances grounded and purposeful.

Your future self will thank you.

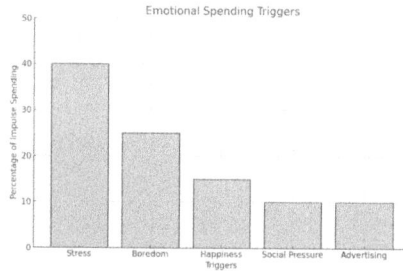

Bar Chart for Emotional Spending Triggers: Highlights common triggers for impulse spending, such as stress and social pressure, to increase awareness.

A budget is often seen as a necessary evil—something you do because you *have* to, not because you *want* to. But after exploring the concepts of mindful budgeting, it should be clear by now: a budget isn't about deprivation or restriction. It's about creating space for what truly matters in your life.

When done mindfully, budgeting becomes less of a chore and more of a tool for empowerment. It's a process that gives you clarity about your finances, helps you align your spending with your values, and allows you to work toward your goals—without sacrificing the joy of living in the moment.

The Journey, Not the Destination

Building a mindful budget isn't a one-and-done task. Life changes, and so do your priorities, income, and expenses. Your budget should grow and evolve with you. Some months will go smoothly, and others might feel like everything went off the rails—but that's okay. What matters is your willingness to adapt and keep moving forward.

Budgeting is a journey, not a destination. It's a skill that improves with practice, reflection, and a healthy dose of curiosity. The key is to approach it with flexibility and compassion for yourself. There's no such thing as the "perfect" budget—there's only the budget that works for you in this moment.

Encouragement for the Road Ahead

As you continue on your financial journey, remember to be kind to yourself. There will be setbacks, impulse buys, and unexpected expenses, but none of these define you. Every mindful choice you make, no matter how small, is a step toward a more intentional and fulfilling financial life.

Think of your budget as a reflection of your values. It's a tool to help you focus on what's important, whether that's saving for the future, enjoying meaningful experiences, or simply living with less stress about money. Celebrate your progress, learn from your challenges, and trust the process.

Key Takeaways

- **A Mindful Budget Aligns Spending with Values and Goals:** By distinguishing between needs, wants, and true desires, you can allocate your resources in a way that reflects what truly matters to you.
- **Distinguishing Needs, Wants, and True Desires is the Foundation of Intentional Financial Choices:** Understanding these categories

allows you to make spending decisions with greater clarity and purpose.

- **Regular Check-Ins Ensure the Budget Adapts to Life's Changes:** Monthly reviews keep your budget flexible and relevant, allowing you to adjust to unexpected events while staying on track.

A Final Word

Your budget isn't just about numbers; it's about your life. It's a way to live with intention, clarity, and confidence, knowing that every dollar you spend or save is aligned with your goals and values.

As you move forward, remember: budgeting is a tool, not a test. You're not aiming for perfection—you're aiming for progress. And with each mindful step, you're creating a financial foundation that supports the life you want to live.

You've got this. Your mindful budget is the start of something powerful, and the best part is, the journey is entirely yours to create.

* * *

TAKE ACTION

Building a Mindful Budget

Challenge: Create a simple budget using the 50/30/20 rule. Track all your expenses for a week to see how your spending aligns with this structure.

* * *

MILESTONE

Celebrate completing your first budget by choosing one financial goal to work toward (e.g., saving for an emergency fund).

* * *

JOURNALLING PROMPTS:

- What are my financial needs, wants, and true desires?
- Does my current spending align with my values and goals? If not, what adjustments can I make?
- How can I set up a budget that feels empowering rather than restrictive?

- What emotions typically drive my spending habits?
- When was the last time I regretted a purchase, and why?
- How can I cultivate gratitude and intentionality in my spending choices?

Chapter 4
The Art of Mindful Spending

I n a world filled with constant advertisements, sales promotions, and societal pressures to "keep up," spending money often becomes an automatic and emotional act. Mindful spending, on the other hand, invites us to pause, reflect, and make choices aligned with our values and goals. This chapter explores how to spend with awareness, how to recognize and counter triggers that lead to unnecessary purchases, and how to cultivate gratitude and intentionality in your financial decisions.

The Essence of Mindful Spending

Mindful spending is about bringing clarity and awareness to your purchasing decisions. It's not about deprivation or rigidly sticking to a budget; it's about understanding what truly matters to you and letting that guide your financial behavior. By cultivating mindful spending habits, you can reduce regret, increase satisfaction, and ensure that your money is working for your priorities—not against them.

. . .

Strategies for Reducing Emotional Spending

Emotional spending often stems from stress, boredom, or the desire to fulfill a deeper, unmet need. Here are some strategies to reduce it:

1. **Pause Before You Purchase**
   - Create a rule for yourself: wait 24 hours before making any non-essential purchase. This cooling-off period can help you distinguish between fleeting desires and true needs.
2. **Identify Emotional Triggers**
   - Reflect on situations that lead you to spend impulsively. Is it stress after a tough day at work? FOMO (fear of missing out) when you see a friend's social media post? Knowing your triggers allows you to approach them with mindfulness instead of reactivity.
3. **Find Non-Financial Coping Mechanisms**
   - Replace the act of spending with other stress-relief activities, such as journaling, walking, or practicing a brief meditation. By addressing the underlying emotion directly, you can break the cycle of emotional spending.
4. **Track Impulse Purchases**
   - Keep a journal of purchases you make on a whim. Note what you were feeling at the time, the circumstances, and whether you felt regret afterward. Over time, patterns will emerge, giving you valuable insights into your spending behavior.

Practicing Gratitude and Intentionality in Purchases

When we shift our mindset to view money as a tool to support our values and well-being, spending becomes more intentional and fulfilling. Here's how to cultivate gratitude and purpose in your financial decisions:

1. **Reflect on the Purpose of Each Purchase**
   - Before spending, ask yourself: *Does this purchase align with my values and priorities?* This simple question can act as a filter, guiding you toward intentional choices.
2. **Celebrate the Act of Spending Wisely**
   - When you make a purchase that aligns with your goals—whether it's paying for a class, investing in quality items, or supporting a cause you care about—acknowledge it as a positive act.
3. **Be Grateful for What You Already Have**
   - Practice gratitude for the possessions and experiences you already enjoy. This reduces the urge to seek satisfaction through new acquisitions.
4. **Invest in Experiences Over Things**
   - Research shows that spending on experiences (like travel or learning) often brings more lasting happiness than material purchases. Experiences enrich your life and often leave behind meaningful memories.

Recognizing Marketing Triggers and Countering Them Mindfully

Marketers are adept at tapping into our emotions to influence spending. By being mindful of their tactics, you can regain control over your decisions.

1. **Spot the Triggers**
   - Common marketing strategies include scarcity tactics ("Only 3 left in stock!"), time pressure ("Sale ends tonight!"), and emotional appeals ("You deserve this!"). Recognize these as deliberate

strategies designed to manipulate urgency and desire.

2. **Create a "No-Buy" Buffer**
   - When you see a tempting offer, give yourself permission to walk away and revisit it later. Often, the urgency diminishes, and you realize the purchase wasn't necessary.

3. **Limit Exposure**
   - Reduce exposure to marketing by unsubscribing from promotional emails, limiting time on shopping apps, and curating your social media feeds to avoid advertisements.

4. **Focus on Your Financial Goals**
   - Keep a visual reminder of your financial priorities— whether it's a savings goal, a vision board, or a simple sticky note on your wallet. Use it as a grounding tool when faced with marketing temptations.

Journaling Exercise: Reflecting on Recent Purchases

Take some time to analyze your recent spending decisions with this simple yet revealing journaling exercise:

1. **List Your Last Five Purchases**
   - Write down the last five things you spent money on, including the amount and reason for the purchase.

2. **Assess the Value**
   - For each purchase, reflect on the following:
     - *Was this purchase aligned with my values and priorities?*
     - *Did this purchase bring me joy, satisfaction, or utility?*
     - *Would I make the same decision again? Why or why not?*

3. **Explore Alternatives**

Jade Harper

- If you feel regret about a purchase, consider what you could have done differently. Could you have delayed the purchase, found a more cost-effective option, or skipped it altogether?

4. **Set an Intention**
   - Write down one intention for future spending based on what you've learned. For example: *"I will pause and reflect before buying items I don't need."*

Building Awareness One Purchase at a Time

The art of mindful spending is not about achieving perfection but about increasing awareness and making small, consistent improvements in your relationship with money. By reducing emotional purchases, practicing gratitude, and countering marketing triggers, you can transform spending into a meaningful act that supports your life goals and values.

With each intentional purchase, you take a step closer to financial peace and balance. In the next chapter, we'll explore how saving and investing mindfully can further empower you to build a secure and value-driven financial future.

* * *

TAKE ACTION

Challenge: Implement a 24-hour pause rule for non-essential purchases and track how many items you avoided buying impulsively.

* * *

42

MILESTONE

Reflect on the purchases you paused and reward yourself by adding the saved money to your goals fund.

* * *

JOURNALLING PROMPTS:

- What emotions typically drive my spending habits?
- When was the last time I regretted a purchase, and why?
- How can I cultivate gratitude and intentionality in my spending choices?

Chapter 5
Mindful Saving and Investing

Saving and investing are often viewed as complex or burdensome tasks, but they can also be transformative acts of self-care and empowerment. When approached mindfully, these financial practices offer a sense of security and alignment with your values, reducing stress and fostering long-term well-being. In this chapter, we will explore how to save and invest mindfully, set meaningful financial goals, and work toward your future with clarity and purpose.

Savings as a Form of Self-Care and Security

Saving money is not just a financial strategy; it's a way to care for your future self. Building a savings cushion provides peace of mind, empowering you to navigate life's uncertainties with confidence.

1. **Reframe Saving as an Act of Kindness**
   o Think of saving not as sacrificing today's enjoyment but as a gift to your future self. This mindset shift can

transform saving from a chore into an act of self-compassion.

2. **Start Small, Build Momentum**
   - Even small, consistent contributions to savings can add up over time. Celebrate these small victories as steps toward greater financial stability.

3. **Create an Emergency Fund**
   - An emergency fund is the cornerstone of financial security. Aim to save three to six months' worth of living expenses, but start with a smaller, achievable goal—like $500 or $1,000—to build confidence.

4. **Tie Savings to Your Values**
   - Consider how saving supports your broader life values. For instance, saving for travel reflects a love of exploration, while setting aside funds for education reflects a value of growth and learning.

Introduction to Mindful Investing

Investing mindfully is about aligning your investments with your financial goals, risk tolerance, and personal values. It's a way to grow your wealth while staying true to what matters most to you.

1. **Understand the Basics**
   - Before diving into investing, educate yourself on key concepts like risk, diversification, and time horizons. This foundational knowledge helps you make informed decisions and reduces anxiety.

2. **Invest According to Your Values**
   - Explore socially responsible or sustainable investing options that align with your beliefs. Whether you prioritize environmental sustainability, social justice, or ethical governance, you can find investment opportunities that reflect your values.

3. **Focus on Long-Term Growth**

- Avoid getting caught up in short-term market fluctuations. A mindful investor takes a long-term view, recognizing that patience is key to building wealth.

4. **Seek Guidance if Needed**
   - If investing feels overwhelming, consider working with a financial advisor who understands your goals and values. Alternatively, use accessible tools like robo-advisors, which can simplify the process while aligning with your risk preferences.

Setting Mindful Financial Goals

Mindful financial goals provide clarity and motivation, ensuring your saving and investing efforts are purposeful and aligned with your aspirations.

1. **Distinguish Between Short-Term and Long-Term Goals**
   - Short-term goals might include saving for a vacation, building an emergency fund, or paying off debt. Long-term goals could involve retirement savings, buying a home, or funding your child's education.

2. **Use the SMART Framework**
   - Goals should be Specific, Measurable, Achievable, Relevant, and Time-bound. For example:
     - *"Save $5,000 for a down payment on a car within 12 months."*

3. **Break Goals into Milestones**
   - Divide larger goals into smaller, manageable steps. For instance, if your goal is to save $12,000 in a year, aim to save $1,000 per month.

4. **Track Progress Mindfully**
   - Regularly review your goals, not with judgment but

with curiosity and compassion. Celebrate your progress and adjust your plans as needed.

Visualizing Future Needs and Working Toward Them Without Stress

Visualization is a powerful mindfulness tool that can help you clarify your aspirations and stay motivated in your saving and investing journey.

1. **Create a Vision Board for Your Financial Future**
   - Use images, words, and symbols to represent your financial goals. Place the vision board somewhere visible to serve as a daily reminder of what you're working toward.
2. **Practice Future-Self Visualization**
   - Close your eyes and imagine your future self enjoying the benefits of mindful saving and investing. Picture the security, freedom, or opportunities this provides. This practice strengthens your emotional connection to your goals.
3. **Embrace Flexibility**
   - While it's important to have a plan, recognize that life is unpredictable. Be open to adjusting your goals and strategies as circumstances change, without guilt or stress.
4. **Focus on Progress, Not Perfection**
   - Financial journeys are rarely linear. Instead of fixating on setbacks, focus on the progress you've made and the lessons you've learned along the way.

A Mindful Savings Plan: Putting It All Together

To illustrate mindful saving and investing in action, consider the following example:

47

1. **Set a Goal:** Save $10,000 for a home down payment in two years.
2. **Identify Values:** Value of stability and providing a safe space for family.
3. **Create a Savings Strategy:** Save $417 per month by automating transfers to a high-yield savings account. Reduce discretionary spending by $100 per month and allocate the difference toward the goal.
4. **Invest Complementarily:** Place any additional savings into a low-risk investment fund aligned with your timeline and values.
5. **Celebrate Milestones:** Celebrate reaching every $2,000 saved with a small reward, like a family outing.

Empowered and Secure Through Mindful Financial Practices

Mindful saving and investing are not about accumulating wealth for its own sake; they're about creating a financial foundation that supports your values, aspirations, and peace of mind. By saving as an act of self-care, investing with intention, and working toward your goals without undue stress, you cultivate a financial life that feels secure, empowering, and deeply aligned with your sense of purpose.

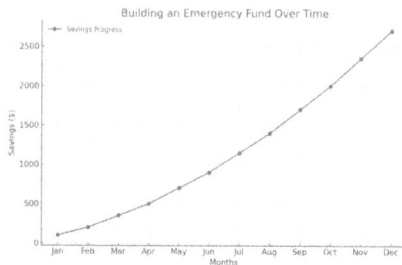

Line Chart for Building an Emergency Fund Over Time: Tracks the progression of savings over a year, demonstrating how consistent contributions lead to a robust financial cushion.

* * *

TAKE ACTION

Mindful Saving and Investing

Challenge: Set a specific savings goal (e.g., $500 for emergencies) and automate a small weekly contribution toward it.

* * *

MILESTONE

Celebrate reaching 10% of your goal by visualizing what achieving the full amount will feel like and treating yourself to something small but meaningful (e.g., a relaxing activity).

Chapter 6
Overcoming Financial Trauma

Money carries emotional weight, and for many, past negative experiences with finances can lead to lasting feelings of fear, shame, or inadequacy. These feelings—known as financial trauma—can shape our financial decisions, behaviors, and even our sense of self-worth. Overcoming financial trauma is not about erasing the past but about finding healing, reclaiming empowerment, and building a healthier relationship with money. In this chapter, we'll explore what financial trauma is, how it manifests, and how mindfulness and practical strategies can help you move forward with confidence and compassion.

Understanding Financial Trauma and Its Long-Term Impact

Financial trauma arises from distressing experiences related to money, such as poverty, debt, job loss, financial abuse, or economic instability during childhood. These experiences can leave deep emotional scars that influence financial behaviors in adulthood.

1. **Signs of Financial Trauma**
   - Chronic anxiety or avoidance about money.
   - Guilt or shame around spending or saving.
   - Overwhelming fear of financial instability, even when financially secure.
   - Difficulty trusting oneself or others in financial matters.
2. **The Psychological Impact**
   - Financial trauma can trigger the brain's fight-or-flight response, making it hard to think clearly about money. It can also lead to limiting beliefs, such as "I'll never be good with money" or "I'll always struggle financially."
3. **How Trauma Shapes Behavior**
   - **Overcompensation:** Excessive saving, hoarding, or workaholism as a way to avoid past financial pain.
   - **Avoidance:** Refusing to check bank balances, ignoring bills, or avoiding financial planning due to fear.
   - **Reenactment:** Repeating unhealthy financial patterns, such as accumulating debt or making risky investments.

Mindfulness-Based Techniques for Dealing with Financial Anxiety and Shame

Mindfulness can help you face financial trauma with curiosity and compassion, creating space for healing and growth.

1. **Acknowledge and Name Your Emotions**
   - Begin by noticing how you feel about money without judgment. Are you anxious, ashamed, or angry? Naming your emotions helps you process them.
2. *Mindfulness Exercise:*

3. Sit quietly and bring your attention to a recent financial situation. Notice the sensations in your body and any thoughts that arise. Breathe deeply and remind yourself: *"This feeling is valid, and I am safe in this moment."*

4. **Separate the Past from the Present**
   o Recognize when your reactions to money are rooted in past experiences. Ground yourself in the present by observing the reality of your current financial situation.

5. *Grounding Practice:*

6. When financial anxiety arises, pause and engage your senses. Describe five things you can see, four things you can touch, three things you can hear, two things you can smell, and one thing you can taste. This practice brings you back to the present moment.

7. **Practice Self-Compassion**
   o Financial trauma often carries a heavy burden of shame. Replace self-criticism with self-kindness by acknowledging that everyone makes financial mistakes or faces challenges.

8. *Mantra for Self-Compassion:*

9. Repeat: *"I am doing the best I can. My worth is not defined by my financial past."*

Practical Steps to Rebuild Trust in Oneself and One's Financial Future

Healing from financial trauma involves not only emotional work but also practical actions to rebuild trust in your ability to manage money.

1. **Start Small and Build Confidence**
   o Begin with manageable financial tasks, such as reviewing a single bank statement or setting aside a

small amount for savings. Celebrate each step as a victory.

2. **Create a Safe Financial Plan**
   - Establish a budget that prioritizes your emotional well-being. Include a category for self-care and set realistic financial goals that don't feel overwhelming.
3. **Seek Professional Support**
   - A financial therapist or counselor can help you address deeper emotional wounds, while a financial advisor can provide practical guidance without judgment.
4. **Establish Financial Boundaries**
   - If financial trauma stems from unhealthy relationships or financial abuse, set clear boundaries to protect yourself. This might include separating finances, creating a budget independent of others, or saying no to financial demands.

Exercises for Forgiving Past Financial Mistakes and Moving Forward

Forgiveness is a critical part of overcoming financial trauma, allowing you to release the weight of past decisions and embrace a new path.

1. **Write a Letter of Forgiveness**
   - Write a letter to yourself about a financial mistake or difficult experience. Acknowledge the circumstances, express understanding, and forgive yourself for any perceived shortcomings.
2. *Example:*
3. *"Dear [Your Name], I forgive you for taking on debt during a tough time. You did the best you could with the resources and knowledge you had. I release this burden*

and commit to moving forward with compassion and wisdom."

4. **Reframe the Narrative**
   o Revisit a painful financial memory and look for lessons or growth. Ask yourself: *What did I learn from this experience? How can I use this knowledge to make better choices?*

5. **Create a Financial Resilience Ritual**
   o Design a ritual to symbolize letting go of financial shame and embracing a fresh start. This might include lighting a candle, journaling, or creating a vision board for your financial future.

6. **Set a New Intention**
   o Choose a mantra or affirmation to guide your financial decisions moving forward. For example:
     - *"I am capable of managing money wisely."*
     - *"I release the past and embrace abundance."*

The Path to Empowerment

Overcoming financial trauma is a journey of self-discovery, healing, and empowerment. By acknowledging your financial wounds, practicing mindfulness, and taking small, intentional steps forward, you can build a healthier and more compassionate relationship with money. Remember, your worth is not tied to your financial history. You have the power to transform your relationship with money and create a future that aligns with your values and aspirations.

In the next chapter, we'll explore how financial mindfulness can strengthen your relationships, fostering open communication and shared goals with loved ones.

$$* * *$$

TAKE ACTION

Overcoming Financial Trauma

Challenge: Write a letter to yourself forgiving past financial mistakes. Identify one step to rebuild trust in your financial decisions.

* * *

MILESTONE

Celebrate this act of self-compassion by creating a financial affirmation you can revisit daily.

* * *

JOURNALLING PROMPTS:

- What past financial experiences have caused me shame or anxiety?
- How can I start to heal from these experiences and forgive myself for financial mistakes?
- What's one small step I can take to rebuild trust in my ability to manage money?

Chapter 7
Money and Relationships

M oney is one of the most common sources of tension in relationships. Whether it's with a partner, family member, or friend, financial conflicts often stem from unspoken expectations, mismatched values, or a lack of communication. Practicing financial mindfulness in your relationships can help reduce conflict, foster trust, and create shared financial harmony. This chapter explores how to communicate mindfully about money, establish healthy boundaries, and align financial goals with loved ones.

The Importance of Financial Communication in Relationships

Open, honest, and respectful communication is the foundation of financial harmony in any relationship. When money is a taboo topic, misunderstandings and resentments can build over time. Mindful communication creates a safe space to discuss finances without judgment or defensiveness.

1. **Approach Conversations with Curiosity**

- Instead of assuming how someone feels about money, ask questions with genuine interest. For example:
  - *"What are your financial priorities right now?"*
  - *"How do you feel about our current financial habits?"*

2. **Choose the Right Time and Place**
   - Money discussions can be emotionally charged. Pick a calm, neutral time to talk, free from distractions or stress. Avoid bringing up financial concerns during an argument or a rushed moment.

3. **Use "I" Statements**
   - Frame your thoughts in a way that expresses your feelings without placing blame. For example:
     - Instead of: *"You spend too much on unnecessary things,"* say, *"I feel anxious when we don't stick to our budget."*

4. **Practice Active Listening**
   - Show that you're listening by repeating back what you hear and validating the other person's perspective. For example:
     - *"It sounds like you're worried about not having enough for emergencies. That makes sense, and I want to work on that with you."*

Setting and Respecting Boundaries Around Joint Finances

Clear financial boundaries help prevent misunderstandings and ensure that everyone's needs and preferences are respected. Whether you share finances or keep them separate, boundaries are essential for healthy relationships.

1. **Define Roles and Responsibilities**
   - Decide who will handle specific financial tasks, such as paying bills, tracking expenses, or researching

investments. This division of labor prevents confusion and ensures accountability.

2. **Discuss Financial Independence**
   - Even in joint financial arrangements, it's important for each person to have some level of financial independence. Agree on how much "personal spending" each person can have without needing to . consult the other.

3. **Set Spending Limits**
   - Create a threshold for discussing larger purchases. For example, you might agree to consult each other before spending more than $200 on non-essential items.

4. **Respect Each Other's Values**
   - Understand that everyone has different financial priorities and spending habits. Respect your partner's or loved one's values, even if they differ from your own.

Exercises for Couples to Align Financial Values and Goals

Shared financial goals are a powerful way to bring alignment and purpose to your relationship. These exercises can help you and your partner identify common ground and create a roadmap for the future.

1. **The Money Values Conversation**
   - Sit down together and discuss the role money plays in your lives. Use prompts like:
     - *"What does financial security mean to you?"*
     - *"What's one thing you'd like to spend more money on and why?"*
     - *"What's your biggest financial fear?"*
2. **Create a Joint Vision Board**

- Gather images and words that represent your shared financial goals—such as buying a home, traveling, or starting a business. Display the board somewhere visible to remind you of your common aspirations.

3. **Set SMART Financial Goals Together**
   - Use the SMART framework to create goals that are Specific, Measurable, Achievable, Relevant, and Time-bound. For example:
     - *"Save $10,000 for a down payment on a house in two years by setting aside $400 per month."*

4. **Monthly Money Check-Ins**
   - Schedule regular meetings to review your finances, celebrate progress, and address any challenges. Use these check-ins as an opportunity to recalibrate your goals and plans as needed.

Practicing Empathy and Compassion in Financial Discussions

Money conversations can evoke strong emotions. Practicing empathy and compassion helps create a supportive environment where both parties feel heard and respected.

1. **Acknowledge Emotions**
   - If your partner or loved one expresses financial stress or anxiety, validate their feelings before jumping to solutions. For example:
     - *"I can see that this is really upsetting for you. Let's work through it together."*

2. **Recognize Personal Histories**
   - Understand that each person's financial beliefs and behaviors are shaped by their unique experiences. Approach differences with curiosity rather than judgment.

3. **Focus on the "We"**

- Frame financial discussions as collaborative rather than adversarial. For example:
    - *"How can we tackle this debt together?"*
    - *"Let's figure out a budget that works for both of us."*
4. **Take Breaks When Needed**
    - If a money discussion becomes too heated, agree to pause and revisit the topic later. Taking time to cool off can prevent miscommunication and hurt feelings.

Cultivating Financial Harmony

Mindful financial practices in relationships are about more than numbers; they're about trust, respect, and shared purpose. By communicating openly, setting healthy boundaries, and aligning your values and goals, you can build a financial partnership that strengthens your connection and reduces conflict.

In the next chapter, we'll focus on practical mindfulness techniques to reduce financial stress and maintain a sense of calm and balance in your financial life.

* * *

TAKE ACTION

Money and Relationships

Challenge: Have a money conversation with a loved one using mindful communication techniques. Discuss shared goals or boundaries.

* * *

MILESTONE

Celebrate by setting one joint financial goal (e.g., saving for a trip) and agreeing on actionable steps toward it.

* * *

JOURNALLING PROMPTS:

☐ How do I feel about discussing money with loved ones?

☐ Are there any financial boundaries I need to set or strengthen in my relationships?

☐ How can I approach financial conversations with more empathy and openness?

Chapter 8
Reducing Financial Stress Through Mindfulness Practices

Financial stress is a universal experience. Whether it's managing debt, handling unexpected expenses, or simply feeling overwhelmed by financial responsibilities, money can often feel like a source of anxiety rather than empowerment. However, mindfulness offers a pathway to navigate financial challenges with calmness, clarity, and confidence.

Mindfulness helps us shift from reactive, fear-based decision-making to intentional, thoughtful approaches to managing money. By integrating mindfulness techniques into your financial life, you can reduce stress, enhance emotional balance, and foster a sense of control over your financial journey.

In this chapter, you'll discover practical mindfulness exercises to address financial anxiety, strategies for fearlessly reviewing your finances, and tips for mindfully coping with unexpected setbacks.

Section 1: Understanding Financial Stress

What Causes Financial Stress

Financial stress often arises from a range of common triggers:

1. **Debt:** Struggling to repay loans or credit cards can create feelings of shame and helplessness.
2. **Income Instability:** Irregular income streams, job loss, or insufficient earnings can lead to constant worry about making ends meet.
3. **Unexpected Expenses:** Unplanned costs, such as medical bills or car repairs, can disrupt even the best-laid financial plans.
4. **Unrealistic Expectations:** Societal pressures to "have it all" or compare your financial situation to others can amplify stress unnecessarily.

The emotional and physical toll of financial stress can be significant:

- **Emotional Impact:** Feelings of shame, anxiety, or frustration often accompany financial challenges. These emotions can erode self-confidence and affect personal relationships.
- **Physical Impact:** Chronic financial stress can manifest as headaches, insomnia, fatigue, or even more serious health conditions, such as high blood pressure.

How Mindfulness Helps

Mindfulness provides tools to break the cycle of financial stress by addressing its root causes and calming the body's stress response. Here's how:

1. **Interrupting the Fight-or-Flight Response:**
   - Financial stress often triggers the fight-or-flight response, making it difficult to think clearly or make rational decisions. Mindfulness techniques, such as deep breathing and meditation, help deactivate this response, restoring a sense of calm.
2. **Enhancing Awareness and Clarity:**
   - Mindfulness encourages you to observe your financial situation without judgment, allowing you to make thoughtful, informed decisions.
3. **Building Resilience:**
   - Through mindfulness, you can cultivate a sense of emotional resilience, making it easier to face financial challenges with composure and confidence.
4. **Reframing Financial Challenges:**
   - Mindfulness helps you view financial difficulties as temporary and manageable, reducing their emotional intensity.

In the following sections, we'll explore actionable mindfulness practices that can help you manage financial stress and regain control over your financial life. By approaching money mindfully, you can transform it from a source of anxiety into a tool for stability and growth.

Section 2: Breathing Exercises, Meditation Techniques, and Body Awareness

Mindfulness practices, including breathing exercises, meditation, and body awareness techniques, are effective tools for managing financial stress. These practices help you stay grounded, calm, and focused, even during challenging financial situations.

Breathing Exercises

1. **Deep Belly Breathing:**
   - *How it works:* Place one hand on your chest and the other on your abdomen. Breathe deeply into your abdomen, allowing it to expand, then exhale slowly. Focus on the sensation of the breath.
   - *Benefits:* Activates the parasympathetic nervous system, calming the body and mind during moments of financial anxiety.

2. **Box Breathing:**
   - *How it works:* Inhale for a count of four, hold the breath for four counts, exhale for four counts, and pause for four counts before repeating.

- *Benefits:* Creates a sense of focus and relaxation, helping you feel centered before tackling financial tasks.

Meditation Techniques

1. **Body Scan Meditation:**
   - *How it works:* Sit or lie down in a comfortable position. Close your eyes and bring your attention to different parts of your body, starting from your toes and moving upward. Notice any tension or discomfort and release it with each breath.
   - *Benefits:* Helps you identify and release physical stress caused by financial anxiety, creating a sense of relaxation and clarity.
2. **Visualization Meditation:**
   - *How it works:* Close your eyes and imagine a scenario of financial peace or success. Picture yourself achieving your financial goals, such as paying off debt or building savings. Focus on the feelings of relief and empowerment.
   - *Benefits:* Shifts your focus from worry to possibility, motivating you to take positive action toward your financial aspirations.

Body Awareness Practices

1. **Progressive Muscle Relaxation:**
   - *How it works:* Tense and then relax each muscle group in your body, starting from your toes and working upward. Pay attention to the sensation of relaxation spreading through your body.
   - *Benefits:* Releases physical tension and creates a sense of calm before engaging in financial activities.

2. **Grounding Techniques:**
   - *How it works:* Use sensory input to stay present. For example, press your feet firmly against the ground, feel the texture of a familiar object, or focus on a specific sound or smell.
   - *Benefits:* Anchors you in the present moment, reducing the mental overwhelm that often accompanies financial stress.

By integrating these mindfulness practices into your routine, you can cultivate a greater sense of peace and control over your financial life. These techniques not only help you manage immediate stress but also build long-term resilience, empowering you to face financial challenges with confidence and clarity.

Section 3: Mindful Approaches to Reviewing Bills and Statements

Reviewing bills and financial statements is an essential part of managing money, yet it's often a source of anxiety for many. The fear of facing financial realities can lead to avoidance, which only exacerbates stress in the long run. By approaching these tasks mindfully, you can transform them from intimidating chores into empowering practices. This section explores strategies for overcoming fear, preparing mindfully, breaking down tasks, and practicing gratitude during financial reviews.

Overcoming Fear of Reviewing Finances

Fear of reviewing finances often stems from avoidance patterns rooted in anxiety, guilt, or shame. Avoidance may feel like a temporary reprieve, but it often leads to greater stress over time. Recognizing and reframing this behavior is key to approaching financial reviews with clarity and confidence.

Recognizing Avoidance Patterns

- Avoidance can take many forms, such as procrastinating on opening bills, skipping online banking logins, or pushing financial tasks to the bottom of your to-do list.
- Acknowledge these patterns without judgment. Recognize them as protective behaviors your mind uses to avoid discomfort.

Reframing Financial Reviews as Empowerment

- Shift your perspective: Instead of seeing financial reviews as burdens, view them as acts of self-care and empowerment.
  - Think of the process as gaining insight into your financial health and taking control of your money.
  - Remind yourself that reviewing finances is an opportunity to make intentional choices that align with your goals.

Preparing Mindfully
Creating a calm, focused environment can make the process of reviewing bills and statements feel less intimidating and more intentional. By preparing mindfully, you set the stage for a positive and empowering experience.

Create a Calming Environment

- Choose a quiet, comfortable space for your financial reviews. Reduce distractions by turning off unnecessary notifications or setting aside a specific time.
- Incorporate calming elements, such as:
  - Lighting a candle or using essential oils to create a soothing atmosphere.
  - Preparing a comforting beverage, like tea or coffee, to enjoy during the process.

o Playing soft, instrumental music to reduce tension.

Use Breathing Exercises

- Begin your financial review with a grounding breathwork exercise to calm your mind and body:
  o Try *deep belly breathing* (inhale deeply into your abdomen, then exhale slowly) to reduce tension.
  o During moments of stress, use *box breathing* (inhale for four counts, hold for four, exhale for four, pause for four) to refocus your thoughts.
- Return to your breath whenever you feel overwhelmed during the review.

Breaking Down the Task

Facing your finances all at once can feel overwhelming, but breaking the task into smaller, manageable steps makes it easier to tackle.

Segment the Process

- Divide your financial review into specific categories, such as:
  o Fixed expenses (e.g., rent, utilities).
  o Variable expenses (e.g., groceries, entertainment).
  o Outstanding debts (e.g., credit cards, loans).
- Focus on one category at a time, completing it fully before moving to the next.

Set Time Limits

- Allocate short, focused sessions for financial reviews (e.g., 20–30 minutes). Use a timer if needed to keep the process manageable.

- If the task feels daunting, commit to reviewing just one or two bills or statements in each session.

Celebrate Progress

- After completing a portion of the review, take a moment to acknowledge your effort. Small celebrations—like enjoying a favorite snack or taking a short walk—can reinforce positive associations with financial tasks.

Practicing Gratitude

Gratitude can transform financial reviews into an uplifting experience, shifting your focus from stress to appreciation. By recognizing the positives in your financial situation, you build a mindset of abundance rather than scarcity.

Acknowledge the Positives

- Celebrate the fact that you're taking proactive steps to manage your money, even if it feels challenging.
- Focus on the small wins, such as:
  - Having the resources to pay a bill.
  - Reducing debt, even by a small amount.
  - Gaining clarity about where your money is going.

Gratitude Reflection Exercise

- After completing your review, take a few moments to write down or reflect on financial aspects you're grateful for. Examples might include:
  - A steady source of income.
  - Opportunities to save, even in small amounts.
  - Support from loved ones in managing finances.
- Reflecting on gratitude can counterbalance the stress of

financial challenges and remind you of the progress you've made.

Closing Thoughts

Reviewing bills and statements doesn't have to be a source of fear or dread. By approaching these tasks mindfully—recognizing avoidance patterns, preparing with intention, breaking the task into manageable steps, and practicing gratitude—you can transform financial reviews into moments of empowerment and clarity. Over time, these practices will help reduce financial anxiety and strengthen your confidence in managing money with mindfulness.

Section 4: Daily Mindfulness Practices to Maintain a Calm Financial Mindset

Building a calm and empowered relationship with money requires consistent practice. By integrating small, daily mindfulness habits into your routine, you can cultivate a steady and positive financial mindset. These practices don't have to be time-consuming; even a few intentional moments each day can make a significant difference. This section introduces four key mindfulness techniques—morning affirmations, mindful spending check-ins, evening gratitude journaling, and midday breathers—to help you maintain financial clarity and reduce stress.

Morning Financial Affirmations

Starting your day with affirmations can set the tone for a positive and empowered money mindset. Affirmations are simple, positive statements that help you focus on your financial strengths and goals, replacing anxiety or doubt with confidence and clarity.

How to Practice Morning Affirmations

1. Choose a quiet moment at the start of your day.
2. Repeat a few affirmations aloud, in your mind, or write them down in a journal.
3. Focus on the meaning behind the words and visualize yourself embodying them.

Examples of Financial Affirmations

- *"I am capable of managing my finances with clarity and ease."*
- *"I make mindful decisions that align with my values and goals."*
- *"I have the power to create financial stability and abundance."*

By practicing affirmations, you'll begin to internalize these beliefs, fostering a sense of control and confidence as you approach financial tasks throughout the day.

Mindful Spending Check-Ins

Mindful spending is the practice of aligning your financial choices with your values and goals. A simple check-in before making purchases can prevent impulsive decisions and promote thoughtful, intentional spending.

How to Pause Before Purchases

1. **Take a Moment:** Before purchasing an item—whether online or in person—pause and take a deep breath.
2. **Ask Yourself:**
   - *Does this align with my values or goals?*
   - *Is this a need, a want, or an impulse?*
   - *How will I feel about this purchase tomorrow, next week, or next month?*

3. **Decide with Intention:** If the purchase aligns with your values and feels necessary, proceed. If not, consider delaying or letting it go.

Benefits of Mindful Spending

- Reduces emotional and impulse purchases.
- Creates space to reflect on your financial priorities.
- Strengthens your sense of control and alignment in financial decisions.

Evening Gratitude Journaling

Ending your day with gratitude helps you focus on the positives in your financial journey, no matter how small. Gratitude journaling rewires your brain to notice progress and abundance rather than stress and scarcity.

How to Practice Gratitude Journaling

1. Set aside 5–10 minutes before bed.
2. Write down 2–3 financial wins or aspects of your financial life that you're grateful for.
3. Reflect on why these moments are meaningful and how they support your financial goals.

Examples of Gratitude Entries

- *"I stayed within my grocery budget this week, and it feels great to stick to my plan."*
- *"I made an extra payment toward my credit card debt today, bringing me closer to being debt-free."*
- *"I'm grateful for the steady income from my job that allows me to save for the future."*

Focusing on gratitude at the end of the day not only improves your financial mindset but also helps you sleep with a sense of peace and accomplishment.

Midday Breathers
Financial thoughts can arise at any time, often leading to stress or distraction. Midday breathers are short mindfulness pauses that help you manage these moments and regain focus.
How to Take a Midday Breather

1. **Pause and Breathe:** When financial worries arise, stop what you're doing and take 3–5 deep, mindful breaths. Focus on the sensation of your breath entering and leaving your body.
2. **Bring Awareness to the Present Moment:** Observe your surroundings using your senses (sight, sound, touch). Ground yourself by feeling your feet on the floor or your hands on your lap.
3. **Acknowledge and Release Financial Thoughts:** Instead of pushing away financial concerns, acknowledge them without judgment. Gently remind yourself, *"I'll address this later when I can focus fully."*

Benefits of Midday Breathers

- Interrupts spiraling financial anxiety.
- Creates a sense of calm and presence, reducing emotional reactivity.
- Helps you refocus on tasks at hand, improving productivity and clarity.

Daily mindfulness practices—whether morning affirmations, mindful spending check-ins, evening gratitude journaling, or midday breathers—help you maintain a calm and balanced financial mindset.

These small, intentional actions create a ripple effect, reducing stress and fostering confidence and clarity in your financial life. By incorporating these practices into your routine, you're not just managing money—you're cultivating peace and empowerment in your relationship with it.

Section 5: Tips for Coping with Unexpected Financial Setbacks Mindfully

Financial setbacks can feel overwhelming, especially when they arise suddenly and disrupt your plans. Whether it's an unexpected medical bill, car repair, or loss of income, these moments can trigger intense emotions and make it hard to see a way forward. Mindfulness offers a way to navigate these challenges with clarity, resilience, and a sense of control. By acknowledging your emotions, focusing on solutions, seeking support, and reaffirming your resilience, you can transform financial setbacks into opportunities for growth.

Acknowledge the Emotional Impact

The first step in coping with financial setbacks is recognizing and accepting your emotional response. Suppressing feelings of frustration, sadness, or fear can intensify stress, while acknowledging them creates space for healing and clarity.

How to Process Your Emotions Mindfully

1. **Name Your Feelings:**
   o Say to yourself: *"I feel anxious," "I feel disappointed,"*

or *"I feel scared."* Naming emotions reduces their intensity and helps you gain perspective.

2. **Allow Yourself to Feel:**
   - Give yourself permission to experience your emotions without judgment. This might involve journaling, talking to a trusted friend, or sitting quietly with your thoughts.

3. **Practice Self-Compassion:**
   - Remind yourself: *"It's okay to feel this way. Financial setbacks happen to everyone, and I am capable of navigating this challenge."*

Focus on Immediate Solutions

Once you've acknowledged your emotions, shift your focus to actionable steps. While it's natural to feel overwhelmed by the bigger picture, breaking the problem into smaller, manageable tasks can help you regain a sense of control.

Steps to Take Action Mindfully

1. **Assess the Situation:**
   - Write down the specifics of the setback. What is the immediate financial need? What resources or options are available?

2. **Prioritize Tasks:**
   - Focus on the most urgent aspects first. For example, if you're facing an unexpected expense, identify how much you need and by when.

3. **Break the Issue into Smaller Tasks:**
   - Instead of trying to solve the entire problem at once, create a step-by-step plan. For example:
     - Call the service provider to negotiate a payment plan.
     - Research ways to cover the expense, such as dipping into savings or selling unused items.

- Adjust your budget to free up funds.

Seek Support

You don't have to face financial setbacks alone. Reaching out to trusted individuals or professional resources can provide guidance, encouragement, and practical solutions.

Ways to Seek Support

1. **Trusted Friends or Family:**
   - Share your situation with someone you trust who can offer emotional support or advice. Often, an outside perspective can help you see options you hadn't considered.
2. **Financial Advisors or Counselors:**
   - Consult a financial advisor or nonprofit credit counseling service for guidance on navigating setbacks and creating a recovery plan.
3. **Mindfulness Groups or Communities:**
   - Join groups focused on mindfulness or financial wellness. Sharing experiences and strategies with others can reduce feelings of isolation and provide motivation.

Reaffirm Financial Resilience

Setbacks are a natural part of any financial journey, and how you respond to them can shape your future financial mindset. Reframing challenges as opportunities for growth can help you move forward with confidence.

Mantras to Foster Resilience

- *"This is a challenge, not a defeat."*
- *"I have overcome difficulties before, and I will overcome this too."*
- *"Every setback is an opportunity to learn and grow."*

Reflect on Past Successes

- Recall a time when you successfully navigated a financial or personal challenge. What steps did you take? How did you grow from the experience? Use this reflection to build confidence in your ability to overcome the current situation.

Unexpected financial setbacks can feel daunting, but mindfulness provides tools to approach them with calm and clarity. By acknowledging your emotions, focusing on actionable solutions, seeking support, and reaffirming your resilience, you can transform challenges into opportunities for growth.

Recap of Key Points

- Mindfulness practices, such as breathing exercises, gratitude journaling, and self-compassion, help reduce the emotional intensity of financial stress.
- Breaking setbacks into smaller, manageable tasks fosters a sense of control.
- Seeking support from trusted individuals or professionals can provide valuable guidance and encouragement.
- Reframing setbacks as opportunities builds emotional resilience and confidence.

Encouraging Action

Start small: Choose one mindfulness practice today—whether it's journaling your emotions, practicing deep breathing, or reflecting on a mantra—and use it to approach a financial task or challenge. Over time, these habits will help you cultivate a calm and empowered mindset, no matter what financial obstacles come your way.

* * *

TAKE ACTION

Reducing Financial Stress Through Mindfulness Practices

Challenge: Practice a 10-minute mindfulness exercise focused on financial stress (e.g., breathing while reviewing bills) daily for a week.

* * *

MILESTONE:

Celebrate by reflecting on the changes in your stress levels and choosing one new mindfulness practice to adopt regularly.

* * *

JOURNALLING PROMPTS:

- What aspects of my finances cause me the most stress?
- How does my body react when I think about or handle financial matters?
- What mindfulness practices can I incorporate into my daily routine to reduce financial stress?

Chapter 9
Aligning Money Habits with Life Values

Introduction: The Value of Values

Imagine your money choices as a reflection of your deepest beliefs about what matters most in life. Aligning financial habits with personal values isn't about earning more or spending less —it's about ensuring your financial decisions bring you closer to the life you want to live. This chapter will guide you in uncovering your core values and reshaping money habits to reflect them.

Identifying Personal Values Through Reflection

Your values are the compass for your financial journey. By clarifying what you truly care about, you can align your financial actions with your ideals. Start by reflecting on the following prompts:

1. **What experiences make you feel fulfilled?**
2. Think about moments in your life that brought you joy or meaning. Were they tied to relationships, freedom, creativity, or security?
3. **What would you like your legacy to be?**

4. How do you want to be remembered? What contributions do you want to make to the world?
5. **Who inspires you, and why?**
6. Consider people you admire and the values they embody —kindness, adventure, stability, generosity, or something else.

Re-Evaluating Financial Priorities

With a clear understanding of your values, you can reassess how your current financial priorities align with them.

- **Needs vs. Wants Revisited**:
- Compare your spending patterns with your identified values. Are you prioritizing essentials that align with your purpose, or are you caught up in habits that don't serve your higher goals?
- **Conducting a Values-Based Spending Audit**:
- Review your bank or credit card statements for the past three months. Highlight expenses that align with your values and those that don't. What patterns emerge?

The Power of Saying "No"

Financial obligations often stem from societal pressures, guilt, or fear of missing out. Practicing mindful boundary-setting is essential to honoring your values:

- **Declining without Guilt**:
- Learn to say no to purchases, contributions, or obligations that don't align with your values. For instance, skipping a trendy gadget or a social outing you don't feel connected to can free resources for what truly matters.
- **Replacing with a "Yes" to Values**:
- Every no to something unaligned is a yes to what matters.

Redirect saved resources toward goals like travel, education, or charity that reflect your values.

Creating a "Money Manifesto"

A Money Manifesto is a personalized guide that captures your financial values and goals. It serves as a living document to remind you of what truly matters when making financial decisions.

Steps to Crafting Your Money Manifesto:

1. **Define Your Top 5 Values**:
2. List the five values that resonate most deeply with you, such as freedom, family, health, or creativity.
3. **Write a Vision Statement**:
4. Craft a brief statement about the role money plays in your ideal life. For example:
5. *"Money is a tool I use to create security for my family, support my community, and experience personal growth."*
6. **Set Clear, Value-Based Intentions**:
7. List actionable commitments aligned with your values. Example:
    - *I will save for a home that reflects my need for stability.*
    - *I will invest in causes that align with my belief in sustainability.*
8. **Review and Revise Regularly**:
9. As your life evolves, so will your values and financial priorities. Revisit your manifesto annually to ensure it reflects your current goals.

Examples of Value-Aligned Money Habits

- **Value: Health**
    - Spend on organic groceries or gym memberships.

- ○ Save for medical insurance or preventive health measures.
- **Value: Family**
  - ○ Prioritize savings for family vacations or education funds.
  - ○ Set aside time and money for quality family activities.
- **Value: Creativity**
  - ○ Budget for art supplies or courses.
  - ○ Invest in creating a workspace that inspires you.

Exercises for Aligning Money with Values

1. **The Weekly Reflection Practice**:
2. At the end of each week, list your purchases and categorize them by values. Reflect on how well your spending aligns with your intentions.
3. **The Visualization Exercise**:
4. Close your eyes and imagine your future self five years from now. What kind of life are you living? What financial choices helped you get there? Use this vision to guide today's decisions.

Conclusion: Living in Harmony with Your Values

When your financial habits align with your core values, every dollar you spend or save becomes a meaningful step toward a life of purpose and fulfillment. Money stops being a source of stress and starts being a tool for living authentically.

By the end of this chapter, you'll have a clearer sense of your priorities, a manifesto to guide your decisions, and the confidence to let your values shape your financial journey.

* * *

TAKE ACTION

Aligning Money Habits with Life Values

Challenge: Write down your top five life values and review your spending over the past month to identify how well your habits align with them.

* * *

MILESTONE:

Create a "Money Manifesto" and celebrate this milestone by committing to one new value-aligned habit.

* * *

JOURNALLING PROMPTS:

- What are my top five life values, and how do my current money habits reflect them?
- Are there any financial commitments or habits I need to let go of to live more in alignment with my values?
- What does a value-aligned financial life look and feel like to me?

Chapter 10
Sustaining Financial Mindfulness for Life

The Journey Beyond the First Steps
Mindfulness is not a destination but a continuous practice. Like any habit, financial mindfulness requires dedication and flexibility to adapt as life evolves. This chapter will equip you with tools and strategies to sustain your financial mindfulness journey, helping you maintain balance, awareness, and empowerment in your relationship with money.

Developing Routines That Support Long-Term Financial Mindfulness

The Power of Routine
Building mindful financial habits requires consistent, intentional actions that become second nature over time. Consider incorporating these practices into your daily, weekly, and monthly routines:

1. **Daily Check-Ins**:
    o Spend a moment each morning to reflect on your

intentions for the day. Will your financial decisions align with your values?

- o Use gratitude to acknowledge what you have and release scarcity-driven thoughts.

2. **Weekly Reviews**:
   - o Dedicate 30 minutes at the end of the week to review spending, savings, and any deviations from your budget.
   - o Celebrate wins, such as resisting an impulse purchase or saving toward a goal.

3. **Monthly Strategy Sessions**:
   - o Assess progress toward financial goals, adjust your budget, and plan for upcoming expenses.
   - o Revisit your Money Manifesto to ensure alignment with your current values.

Tools to Maintain Consistency

- **Journaling**: Keep a financial mindfulness journal to track reflections, wins, and lessons.
- **Apps and Alerts**: Leverage budgeting or goal-setting apps to stay on track and receive reminders for mindful spending.
- **Accountability Partners**: Share your progress and plans with a trusted friend or partner for support and encouragement.

Setting Up Regular Financial Check-Ins

Check-Ins with Yourself

Taking time to pause and assess your financial situation regularly can help prevent mindless habits and maintain focus on your goals.

1. **Quarterly Reviews**:

- Reflect on major life changes, shifting priorities, or new opportunities.
- Identify areas where you may need to realign your habits.

2. **Annual Reflection and Reset**:
   - Look back on the past year: What worked? What didn't?
   - Celebrate your progress and redefine goals for the year ahead.

Check-Ins with a Partner

For those sharing financial responsibilities, regular check-ins can enhance communication and reduce misunderstandings:

1. **Monthly Money Dates**:
   - Create a calm, distraction-free environment to review joint finances.
   - Discuss shared goals and any concerns or adjustments needed.
2. **Setting Boundaries and Expectations**:
   - Clearly define roles and responsibilities to avoid conflicts.
   - Use empathetic, nonjudgmental language to foster trust and collaboration.

Reinforcing Positive Financial Habits

Habit-Building Strategies

- **Automation**:
- Automate savings, bill payments, and investments to remove the burden of decision-making and ensure consistency.
- **Reward Systems**:

- Reinforce good habits by treating yourself (mindfully!) when you reach a milestone. For example, celebrate paying off debt with a small, values-aligned reward.
- **Track Your Progress**:
- Use visual tools like graphs or charts to monitor your journey. Seeing tangible progress can motivate you to stay on track.

Reassessing Goals Annually

Life changes, and so do your financial needs and priorities. Take time each year to review and revise your:

- **Short-Term Goals**: Are they still relevant, or do they need adjustment?
- **Long-Term Aspirations**: Are you on track, or should you recalibrate timelines and strategies?
- **Values Alignment**: Have your core values shifted? How should this influence your financial plans?

Mindful Goal-Setting for the Future
Setting Flexible and Compassionate Goals

Financial goals should inspire, not overwhelm. Use these principles to set goals that honor both your ambitions and your humanity:

1. **SMART Framework**:
   - Make goals Specific, Measurable, Achievable, Relevant, and Time-bound.
2. **Build in Flexibility**:
   - Allow for unexpected changes in your life. For example, if saving for a house becomes less urgent due to a job relocation, adjust accordingly without guilt.
3. **Focus on the Journey, Not Just the Destination**:

○ Celebrate each step toward your goal, no matter how small. For instance, each dollar saved for retirement is a win worth acknowledging.

Compassionate Adjustments

Life can throw curveballs—unexpected expenses, changes in income, or shifts in priorities. Approach these situations with self-compassion:

- **Avoid Blame**: Recognize that setbacks are natural and don't define your worth.
- **Refocus**: Reevaluate your goals and create a new plan that fits your current circumstances.
- **Seek Support**: Reach out to a financial advisor, mentor, or supportive friend for guidance.

Conclusion: A Lifetime of Mindful Money Habits

Sustaining financial mindfulness requires commitment, patience, and adaptability. By developing supportive routines, maintaining regular check-ins, and staying flexible with your goals, you can ensure your money habits evolve alongside your life.

Financial mindfulness is a journey, not a destination. With each mindful choice, you'll deepen your understanding of what money can do for you—not as a source of stress, but as a tool for living a life aligned with your values.

Let this chapter, and this book, serve as a resource you return to as you navigate your ongoing relationship with money. Choose awareness, compassion, and intentionality every step of the way. Your financial future is not just about numbers—it's about living a life you truly value.

* * *

TAKE ACTION

Sustaining Financial Mindfulness for Life

Challenge: Schedule a monthly financial check-in with yourself or a partner to review goals and adjust strategies.

* * *

MILESTONE

Celebrate your first check-in by acknowledging your progress and rewarding yourself with a small treat aligned with your values (e.g., a favorite book or quality time with a loved one).

* * *

JOURNALLING PROMPTS:

- What routines or practices have helped me maintain financial mindfulness so far?
- How can I ensure my financial goals and habits evolve as my life changes?
- What's one long-term financial goal I want to focus on, and how can I approach it with intention and flexibility?

Afterword: An Invitation to Mindful Abundance

The journey to financial mindfulness is not about arriving at a fixed destination. Instead, it is a practice that evolves as we grow, as our circumstances shift, and as our understanding of ourselves deepens. Each chapter of this book was designed to guide you in building a foundation of awareness and intentionality, but the true value lies in how you adapt these principles to your unique life.

Money is a Mirror

Our relationship with money often reflects our inner world—our fears, our desires, our beliefs about what is possible. By choosing to approach money mindfully, we grant ourselves the opportunity to uncover and heal these inner dynamics. We begin to see money not as a source of stress or control but as a tool that can support a life aligned with our values.

Financial Peace Beyond Numbers

True financial peace is not found in the size of a bank account or the perfection of a budget. It resides in how we engage with money: with clarity, compassion, and purpose. It's about making choices that reflect who we are and who we aspire to become. It's about reducing fear, cultivating gratitude, and finding empowerment in even the smallest steps forward.

Living Fully and Freely

This is your invitation to live a life of mindful abundance. By viewing money as a means rather than an end, you free yourself from the pressure of external comparisons and align with the richness of your own values. Money becomes a resource to create, connect, and contribute in ways that bring meaning and fulfillment.

As you continue this journey, remember:

- **Be Patient**: Change takes time. Celebrate small wins, and give yourself grace during setbacks.
- **Stay Curious**: Your financial story will evolve. Keep asking questions, exploring possibilities, and refining your practices.
- **Honor Yourself**: Every mindful choice you make is a testament to your commitment to your well-being and future.

A Lifelong Practice

Financial mindfulness is not a static skill—it is a lifelong practice. It requires attention, care, and the willingness to adapt. But with each step, you will discover not just financial clarity, but a deeper connection to your life's purpose and priorities.

Thank you for allowing this book to be a part of your journey. May it serve as a guide, a companion, and a reminder that financial freedom is not about perfection but about living in harmony with what truly matters to you.

Bonus chapter
Mindful Philanthropy – Giving with Intention and Purpose

Mindful Philanthropy – Giving with Intention and Purpose

In a world often driven by accumulation, mindful philanthropy reminds us of the profound joy in giving. When approached with intention, philanthropy can align with our values, enhance our sense of purpose, and contribute to a more equitable and compassionate society. This chapter explores how to give mindfully—whether through money, time, or resources—and how this practice can deepen our connection to ourselves and our communities.

What is Mindful Philanthropy?

Mindful philanthropy is the practice of giving thoughtfully and intentionally, ensuring that your contributions align with your core values and have a meaningful impact. Unlike impulsive or obligatory donations, mindful giving involves careful reflection on:

- **What you give**: Money, time, skills, or tangible resources.

- **Why you give**: The motivations and values driving your philanthropy.
- **How you give**: Ensuring that your contributions are impactful and aligned with both your resources and the needs of others.

Mindful philanthropy is not about how much you give but about giving in a way that feels authentic, sustainable, and fulfilling.

Benefits of Mindful Philanthropy

1. **Fulfilling Your Values**: By giving to causes that resonate with your personal beliefs, you create a sense of alignment between your actions and your life purpose.
2. **Strengthening Community**: Contributions— whether monetary or otherwise—help build stronger, more connected communities.
3. **Boosting Well-Being**: Studies show that giving activates the brain's reward centers, fostering happiness and reducing stress.
4. **Creating a Ripple Effect**: Mindful giving inspires others to contribute, amplifying the impact of your generosity.

How to Practice Mindful Philanthropy
1. Clarify Your Values

Start by identifying what matters most to you. Ask yourself:

- What issues or causes ignite my passion?
- What kind of world do I want to help create?
- How can I use my resources to reflect these priorities?

For example, if environmental sustainability is a key value, you might support organizations focused on conservation or renewable energy.

Action: Write down your top three values and list causes or organizations that align with each.

2. Assess Your Resources

Philanthropy isn't limited to financial contributions. Reflect on the resources you can offer, including:

- **Money**: Regular donations, one-time gifts, or crowdfunding campaigns.
- **Time**: Volunteering, mentoring, or attending events.
- **Skills**: Offering expertise in areas like marketing, teaching, or strategic planning.
- **Tangible Goods**: Donating clothes, food, or supplies.

Example: A busy professional might lack time but can set up a recurring donation, while someone with flexible hours could volunteer at a local shelter.

3. Research and Reflect

Before contributing, take time to learn about the organization or cause:

- Is it reputable and transparent?
- How does it use its resources to create impact?
- Does its mission resonate with your values?

Action: Spend 15 minutes researching a cause that interests you. Reflect on how supporting it aligns with your goals.

4. Create a Giving Plan

Treat philanthropy as an intentional part of your financial or time budget:

- **Set a budget**: Decide what portion of your income you can sustainably allocate to charitable giving.
- **Prioritize consistency**: Smaller, regular contributions often have a greater long-term impact than sporadic large donations.
- **Include non-monetary giving**: Schedule time for volunteering or offering skills to causes you care about.

Example: "I will donate 5% of my income annually to education and volunteer 10 hours a month at a local tutoring program."

5. Give with Presence

When giving, approach the act with mindfulness:

- Reflect on the impact your contribution will have.
- Feel gratitude for the opportunity to make a difference.
- Avoid expectations of recognition; focus on the intrinsic joy of giving.

Mindful Practice: Before donating, take a moment to breathe deeply and visualize the positive ripple effects your contribution will create.

Overcoming Common Barriers to Giving

1. **"I Don't Have Enough to Give"**
   - Solution: Focus on non-monetary resources, like time or skills. Even small contributions can make a big difference.
2. **"I Don't Know Where to Start"**
   - Solution: Begin with causes that resonate with your personal experiences or passions.
3. **"Will My Contribution Really Make an Impact?"**

○ Solution: Research organizations to ensure their values and practices align with yours. Trust that every mindful act of giving contributes to positive change.

The Ripple Effect of Mindful Philanthropy

Your mindful giving can inspire others to contribute, creating a broader movement of intentional generosity. Whether it's encouraging friends to join you in volunteering or sharing your story of supporting a cause, your actions can multiply their impact.

Example: A family who mindfully gives to local food banks might inspire their neighbors to organize a community-wide food drive.

Mini-Challenge: Reflect and Act

1. Identify one cause that deeply resonates with your values.
2. Decide how you want to contribute—whether through money, time, or resources.
3. Take one mindful action this week, such as making a donation, volunteering, or researching organizations to support.

Milestone: Celebrate Your Giving

At the end of the month, reflect on the impact of your contributions. Celebrate the sense of connection and fulfillment that comes from aligning your resources with your values. Reward yourself by engaging in a meaningful activity that brings you joy, like spending time in nature or with loved ones.

By practicing mindful philanthropy, you can transform the act of giving into a profound and joyful expression of your values. When done with intention, philanthropy is not just about helping others—

it's about enriching your own life with purpose, compassion, and connection.

FaQs and Troubleshooting: Starting Your Journey with Financial Mindfulness

Embarking on the path of financial mindfulness can be empowering, but it's natural to encounter questions and challenges along the way. This section addresses some of the most common concerns to help you stay motivated and overcome obstacles.

1. What if I don't have enough money to save or budget?

It's a common concern that budgeting and saving only apply to those with disposable income. However, financial mindfulness is about becoming aware of where your money goes and aligning your spending with your values—regardless of how much you have. Start by tracking your expenses for a week to identify areas where you might cut back, even small amounts. Savings can begin with as little as $1 a week; the habit is more important than the amount.

2. How do I stay consistent with mindful spending?

Consistency can be challenging, especially when life gets busy. Try these strategies:

- **Set reminders:** Use phone alarms or calendar notifications for weekly budget reviews.
- **Practice reflection:** Before each purchase, pause and ask, "Does this align with my values and goals?"
- **Keep it visual:** Place your financial goals where you can see them daily—on your fridge, phone background, or journal. Remember, progress is more important than perfection. If you slip, use it as an opportunity to learn rather than to judge yourself.

3. What if my partner or family isn't on board with these practices?

Discussing money with loved ones can be sensitive. Here's how to approach the conversation:

- **Lead by example:** Share your positive experiences with financial mindfulness, such as reduced stress or progress toward goals.
- **Find common ground:** Identify shared financial priorities (e.g., saving for a vacation or paying off debt).
- **Use "I" statements:** Frame the conversation around your journey rather than criticizing their habits ("I'm trying this new approach to reduce stress," rather than "You're bad with money"). If resistance persists, focus on your own practices while maintaining open communication.

4. How do I overcome emotional spending habits?

Emotional spending often stems from stress, boredom, or the need for comfort. Address it by:

- **Identifying triggers:** Keep a journal to note when you feel the urge to spend impulsively and what emotions are involved.

- **Replacing habits:** Find non-monetary ways to address these emotions, such as taking a walk, meditating, or calling a friend.
- **Implementing a pause rule:** Wait 24 hours before making non-essential purchases. This allows time to reflect on whether the item truly aligns with your values.

5. What if financial trauma from the past makes it hard to engage with money?

Financial trauma can create fear, shame, or avoidance. Start small:

- **Set achievable goals:** Focus on one aspect of your finances, such as reviewing your bank statements weekly.
- **Practice self-compassion:** Acknowledge that past experiences don't define your future, and it's okay to move forward at your own pace.
- **Seek support:** Consider working with a therapist or financial coach who specializes in trauma-informed care.

6. How do I handle unexpected financial setbacks?

Unexpected expenses can disrupt even the best-laid plans. Respond mindfully by:

- **Breathing first:** Use deep breathing techniques to stay calm and avoid reactive decisions.
- **Reassessing priorities:** Temporarily redirect funds from less critical areas to cover the setback.
- **Learning from the experience:** Reflect on how you might prepare for similar situations in the future, such as building an emergency fund.

7. What if mindfulness feels overwhelming or time-consuming?

Mindfulness doesn't have to be a time-consuming practice. Start with simple actions:

- **Set aside five minutes:** Begin with brief exercises, like pausing to reflect before spending or reviewing your goals once a week.
- **Incorporate mindfulness into daily life:** Combine practices with existing habits, such as reflecting on gratitude while brewing coffee.
- **Be kind to yourself:** Remember that mindfulness is a practice, not a perfection. Small, consistent steps lead to meaningful change.

8. How do I maintain momentum over time?

Sustaining financial mindfulness is about creating habits that fit your life:

- **Celebrate wins:** Recognize and reward yourself for milestones, no matter how small.
- **Review regularly:** Schedule monthly check-ins to reflect on your progress and adjust goals as needed.
- **Stay inspired:** Revisit this book, connect with like-minded communities, or listen to podcasts on financial mindfulness to keep your motivation high.

Milton Keynes UK
Ingram Content Group UK Ltd.
UKHW051855051224
452013UK00021B/378

9 783990 955000